With love to carol,

Soli Deo Gloria~

ann

Scripture taken from the
HOLY BIBLE, NEW INTERNATIONAL VERSION.
Copyright 1973, 1978, 1984 by International Bible Society.
Used by permission of Zondervan. All rights reserved.

ISBN 978-0-9791140-0-7

www.workofthelord.com

ann@workofthelord.com

THE WORK
OF
THE LORD

Amelia Island, Florida

Located right on the Atlantic coast of Florida, Amelia Island
has served as my family's summer retreat for over 20 years.
It is where we go to meet with family, rekindle memories of
generations, and renew our souls. Upon reflection, I have
found that my emotional renewal depends on my visit there.
Amelia is a second home for me. Undoubtedly, Amelia is
"Paradise on Earth." After countless summers, I still find
myself in complete awe of its ever-present splendor. Like most
houses by the sea, the most familiar taste and smell is the salty
air. The heat of the sun combined with the salty mist of the
ocean's spray creates an almost sticky paste on my skin.

Amelia is set apart from any other memory in my mind because
of its extravagant beauty. Ancient trees shadow the winding
roads and bike paths. On clear days the brilliant sun sparkles
through a thick canopy of Spanish moss and creates emerald
green patterns on the darkened pavements. Afternoon storms
often ignite chaotic friction between tossing oak branches,
scattering fallen debris in all directions. The disarray of the
storm threatens the calmness of the marsh. Serving as one of
Amelia's borders, the intercoastal marsh creates its own
splendor. The tall marsh grass conceals the quiet stream of

salty waterway. Tiny crabs scamper from beneath my feet as great blue herons soar above my head. The air is still and silent, only to be interrupted with the serenade of crickets and frogs. The serenity of the marsh mirrors the tranquility of the shore. The waves spill white foam as they tumble onto the packed sand. Sandpiper families frantically dig for food before the water challenges their pursuit. Pelicans gracefully skim the water, forming to the shape of the rising swells. Amelia's wide, white beach sets it apart from any other beach resort area. Shell piles decorate the clean sand. The orange and pink sunset, vibrating with life, yields the sky to a black blanket of stars that drapes the moon-reflecting ocean. Dawn brings the morning sun and a new day to experience life in paradise.

The island was named in 1736 by English settlers after Princess Amelia, daughter of King George. "Amelia" is a German word meaning "The Work of the Lord." The island was named to celebrate Princess Amelia's natural beauty. The splendor of the seashore and intercoastal marshland is a fitting tribute. For three generations, my family has celebrated the work of the Lord through the beauty of Amelia.

To Mom and Dad:
You "live a life of love" (Ephesians 5:2).
Thank you for teaching me to
cherish my faith, embrace this dream,
and adore the beach.

With Gratitude

"A longing fulfilled is sweet to the soul" (Proverbs 13:19). The words printed here cannot do justice to the gratitude that fills my heart. My journey with *The Work of the Lord* has been inspired, encouraged, and prayed over by many.

To the dear friends who have shared in this adventure, thank you. The beauty of the Lord's creation was magnified in this book thanks to the talent and dedication of Marianne Kershaw. You have helped me create my dream. I am grateful for the careful editing of Dianna Melson and Robby Higginbottom. You have given my words renewed life.

With heartfelt appreciation to my precious family: Mom, Dad, Jed, Ellen, John, the Longs, and the Melsons. You are the reason my cup brims with blessings. May this book be a reflection of our shared lives.

With gratitude to the Lord: my resplendent inspiration. May the words and photographs that fill these pages captivate hearts for Your glory. Your splendor is my song…thank You for writing the lyrics of my heart.

Contents

Preface

Life on an island overwhelms me with transcendent time, beauty, and revelation. Just being there inspires the soul. Memories of laughter, a favorite song, or a story told embrace the heart once again with distant thoughts and brief pleasures. Magical. Taking in the familiar surroundings leads to powerful self-renewal and sharpens the senses to a new awakening. Spiritual. God's glory is mirrored in nature's passion of color and aroma. Timeless. A moment is captured to stand the test of time's erosion. Harmony.

I blend into the island. It seems like a physical extension of myself as I feel the rhythm of the message it retells just for me. Amelia. An ancient island of enchantment that summons me to stay, to remember its spirit, and to treasure this special place in my heart.

For those of you who frequent the beach, use this as an oceanside devotional. Carry it in your beach bag, and read it with your toes in the sand. Explore the character of the Lord as exemplified in His creation at the beach. Spread out your beach towel, and soak in the Son.

Perhaps you live in the city or you have never experienced the seashore. Allow God to draw you away to spend time in His presence. You have been gifted with an imagination. Close your eyes, listen for the ocean's roar, and escape to the serenity by the sea. It is not necessary to be on an actual beach to encounter God's character through His creation. Be carried away out of traffic and into communion with the Lord—to an oceanside retreat.

His Blessings
Bountiful Blessings

*"Since you are precious
and honored in My sight,
and because I love you…"*
~ Isaiah 43:4

You are the work of His hand
and His greatest delight. In the
moment of creation, YOU were
the finishing touch. After the
stars were scattered in the sky
and the mountains were perfectly
peaked, He created each one
of us. The Lord's delight in us
is revealed through bountiful
blessings.

The beach is filled with
blessings, and what is more, they
are specific to the individual.
This morning, I see those
blessings in abundance. I wrote
the following after reflecting
on the coast's greatest—and
sometimes most simple—
blessings. Our God is a
God of personal touch and
overwhelming love. Notice
the most infinite detail of a
shell… or the grandeur of the
mighty ocean…and listen as the
Creator sings a song of blessing.

Since you are precious and honored in My sight,
I want to shower you with blessings.
Because I love you with an everlasting love,
I want to show you things you only dream of.
In the morning, look over the ocean.
See the sun hit the shore, and feel blessed.
Awaken to a new day filled with endless possibilities,
And know you are richly blessed.
I have given you a family.
And through them, I have shown you love as I designed it.
I have surrounded you with ambassadors of My kingdom—
Be blessed in their teaching.
I have purposefully placed you in the life of others…
So that your life may overflow into theirs,
Leaving a trail of blessings.
Notice the little things in your life that make you smile.
A smile, a hug, an opportunity…
They are gifts from Me, created for you.
Nature sings of My blessings.
A beautiful day is full of intention.
A peaceful ocean, a gentle breeze, the great blue heron…
These were created by Me,
Because I knew how you would love them.
Delicate flowers and sand dollars…
I put them in your path to please you.
I want to bless you.

A dark night's shooting star was commissioned as a blessing…
My way of reassuring your questioning heart.
Wait for what I want to show you today—
As I call you to feel My love like no other day before.
I will reveal Myself to you
In a way that is unmistakably divine.
I have a great plan.
And beloved, I purposed to love you before time began.
For you I sent my Son, to secure you by My side.
I have chased your heart, to embrace you with blessings—
Blessings designed to uphold you and bring you peace.
Listen to your desires.
I know what is written on your heart,
For I wrote the lyrics of your song.
The sunset makes your heart take flight,
So notice there is one every day and in your favorite colors.
Feel blessed when you are with those you love.
Feel blessed when you are doing what you love.
Feel blessed when you see beauty that takes your breath away.
Feel blessed when you lay your head down to sleep.
Count the ways I have rejoiced over you today,
And anticipate the ways in which I will bless you tomorrow.
Because I love you,
And because you are My most cherished creation,
I will brim your cup with blessings.

His Calling
Whispering Call

"The Lord said, 'Go out and stand on the mountain in the presence of the Lord, for the Lord is about to pass by.' Then a great and powerful wind tore the mountains apart and shattered the rocks before the Lord, but the Lord was not in the wind. After the wind there was an earthquake, but the Lord was not in the earthquake. After the earthquake came a fire, but the Lord was not in the fire. And after the fire came a gentle whisper..."
~ I Kings 19:11-12

I have come to know the Lord to be subtle in His call. Similar to Elijah, I often wait for obvious signs. Shattered rocks and earthquakes grab my attention. In fact, sometimes I am so busy waiting for a shout, that I miss the gentle whisper. This morning I woke up with a sense of urgency. The stillness of the dawn captured my attention. My time on the beach inspired a rush of thoughts. Waiting for the sun to hit the horizon, I came to understand a characteristic of the Lord: His gentleness.

Listen for the quiet call of the Lord. Sometimes His greatest lessons and most poignant guidance come in the form of a whisper. He has a calling for your life. Have you listened intently to discover it? What noise distracts you from hearing His call? To what are you listening? Do not limit yourself to the powerful wind or the fierce fire. Some grace-given assignments echo in the softness of a whisper.

Between the fading stars and dawning in the new day's light
A time of simple stillness calls me out of lingering night.
Before the buzz of life, I'm rising, stirring from my bed,
Now wide awake and to the shore, the place my heart is led.
Quietly I listen for the whisper that will teach.
Barefoot, I with open heart, in silence stroll the beach.
While feet brush into shells, my soul is touched by His own hand—
A morning ordinary? No, but rather something grand.
The shoreline sweeps beyond the bend, traced by a single bird.
The scene before my eyes: an ocean speaks the Living Word.

Humbled by His beauty and the sea breeze gentle kiss,
My heart pours forth its joyful song and fills with graceful bliss.
Today stands here before me; I won't let this moment fall.
Tomorrow is uncertain; faith today must heed the call.
Lord, make me Your song's instrument and show me where to play,
And like this morning, cover me with warmth of guiding ray.
I yearn for overwhelming sound, for evidence to show;
Your gentle whisper echoes all I'll ever need to know
Of promises and faithfulness. Your perfect record cries
That we can trust the gentle voice that takes us by surprise.

Bring joy to me, oh gracious King, I give You back Your day.
Creator of this glorious morn, each step, reveal the Way.
I rest upon Your providence, yet diligently seek
The stillness that I need if Lord, I hope to hear You speak.
With eyes on Your horizon and my heart exulting high,
I drink in so much beauty: Your world wakes and starts to fly.
Waves are rolling gently, crashing right here where I stand.
The whisper on the water reaches my uplifted hand.
This is the day that You have made, each moment's detail known;
Tomorrow is not mine to fear, for I am called Your own.

The quiet morning, changing color, soon will dance with light,
I turn and walk the sand towards home, enthralled by heavenly sight.
And back of me the day begins with warmth from radiant ball:
Another day to trust the timing of His whispering call.

His Compassion
Morning Compassions

"Because of the Lord's great love, we are not consumed, for His compassions never fail. They are new every morning; great is Your faithfulness."
~ *Lamentations 3:22-23*

My favorite part of the day is right before it even begins. The earth is still dark, the world is sleeping, and I feel as though I am alone with my Creator. He met me early this morning, a little shy of 6:00 am. Today, among all days, was different. He wanted me awake. There would be much to see—*"Things,"* He said, *"that I don't want you to miss."* I sat in the silence of the morning, scanning the beach for others. I came to the conclusion that I was part of a select audience for the sky's most spectacular performance: sunrise over the water. For a moment, the world stops its constant motion. All of nature holds its breath as a tiny sliver of bright orange peeks over the horizon. Gradually, it climbs over the line, bursting with more and more radiance with each passing second. Oh Father, I fear that I might blink and miss a moment of this glorious presentation. Brilliant shades of pink, orange, and yellow slowly streak the sky, outlining the clouds before exploding all over creation. Colors dance across the water, forming a lingering pathway to the shore. They glaze the surf before blushing my face. Lost in amazement, I wonder at the creativity of our God who faithfully gives us an original sunrise every morning.

Glorious God, Your faithfulness is exemplified in the rising of the sun. You are the light of the world and in every manner, You are the light of my life. In a cold and

dark world, You light the path. You give us illumination to follow in Your way.

Through nighttime and darkness, we stumble. There are times when nothing makes sense, and life tells us that it is hopeless. No longer is the road clearly laid out, and we cannot see the next step, let alone what lies farther ahead. It is by faith that we wait for light…and then it comes. Ever so slowly, yet in all perfection, the sun creeps over the horizon, and our path is lit. From dawn until dusk, there is enough light to see our feet, enough light to make sense of this dark world. The Lord provides a sun to bring clarity and help us make sense of the physical world; and the Lord provides a Son to bring clarity and make sense of everything. And without the Son, we dwell in darkness.

So there is just enough light for one day…and then the sun sinks and darkness sweeps over. And we wait in great faith and expectation that it will come again in the morning. A new day begins. Because of the Lord's great love, we are not consumed by the darkness, for His compassions never fail. Praise the Lord that they are new every morning! Every morning I am in desperate need of them, and because of His faithfulness, compassions rain down with the rising of the sun.

Life does not make a lot of sense when it is dark. I am so quick to rely on my own strength, so quick to lose my perspective. I push through the darkness of confusion, complacency, frustration, and exhaustion. And just before I lose my step, I am showered in His splendor and my world has light. Lord, we are dependent on Your light and in desperate need of a sunrise each and every morning.

You provide everything we need and more. You provide it all in abundance. Not only do You provide the light, but You provide it in a breathtaking sunrise that captivates our souls. You alone are glorified in the morning light.

It amazes me that most of the world sleeps through the most magnificent moments of the day. I am ashamed that I often miss them as well. But in the quietness of this particular morning, I hear Him whisper,

"Wake up, My beloved one. Today you will see Me as never before. I have created a sight more spectacular than you can ever imagine. No artist can capture what I have created for you this morning. I never intended for you to walk in darkness, so let Me give you light. And because I love you deeply, I have created the sunrise with brilliant colors and warm rays. Watch and be amazed, for My compassions are brand new this morning and are yours for the entire day. When the sun sets tonight, and when your life is no longer clear, know dear child, that it is only because I want you to trust Me. I want you to take My hand and secure your faith in who I am. For I am the way, the truth, and yes, My love, I am the life. Walk in faith, even when you cannot see. Remember that, on what seemed like the darkest day, My Son rose from the darkness to bring light and life to those who would believe. You can trust Me. In the morning I will give you enough light for yet another day."

It is perfectly fitting with the character of our Gracious Father that His faithfulness arrives in such splendor. No camera can capture what my soul has tasted this morning. In darkness I waited until a palate burst forth and heaven boldly exclaimed,

"Do you like it? I made it just for you..."

His Everpresence
I Am

"I am who I am."
~ Exodus 3:14

The Lord's character is not easily defined. He is not limited to
one location or one situation. I love C.S. Lewis' thought: "I
believe in Christ like I believe in the sun; not because I see it,
but because by it I can see everything else." Through Him, we
are able to see all. The most magnificent part of the Lord is
that He cannot be contained. He is here…and He is there.
His everpresence is unmistakable.

If I go up to the heavens, You are there;
If I make my bed in the depths, You are there.
If I rise on the wings of the dawn,
If I settle on the far side of the sea,
Even there Your hand will guide me,
Your right hand will hold me fast.
~ Psalm 139:8-10

We should not worry about tomorrow, for He is already there.
Look up and down the beach. He is in every detail. Celebrate
the Lord's presence!

I knew each day before one came to be, so today,
I am here.
In the quiet of the morning, while you softly sleep, I am awake.
I am there.
When the sun rises, when the clouds fill with color,
I am there.

As the pelican rides the wind, as the dolphin leaps for joy,
As the child builds a sandcastle, as the old man strolls the surf,
I am there.
When your grandmother's smile warms your heart,
When your grandfather's touch calms your fears,
I am there.
When you watch your cousins play,
When you hear your sister laugh,
I am there.

Try to count the grains of sand in your hand,
And know that I am.
Notice the infinite detail of each shell:
I am the designer of each line and curve.
When you see the faithfulness of the waves,
When you feel the gentleness of the wind, remember Me.
I am there.
In the thunder's distant rumble, in its echo's piercing call,
In the might of raging water, in storms so fierce then calm,
Know that I am who I am.
In the rainbow's arc read My promise of compassion
And remember that I am.
When the sun sets with its palate of splendor,
I am there.
I am in the room filled with family,
I am magnified in each hug and loving remark.

I am among you as you hold hands,
When you ask for a blessing, in My abundance,
I am there.

As you count the stars, I am calling them by name.
When the moon glows, when the night is dark,
I am there.
I am your heart's deepest desire. When you call My name,
I am there.
As you whisper prayers of concern, I am listening.
As you plead for relief, I am healing.
When you shout offerings of praise, I am rejoicing.
When you drift to sleep, I am sustaining you.
When your eyes shut at last, I am awake,
For I will never leave you nor forsake you.
You need not fear tomorrow, for I am already there.

I am your God, and you are My beloved child.
I will be your vision...I am all you long to see.
I will be your best thought...I'm the highest you can think.
I will have no rival...I want first place in your heart.
I offer sleep to those I love and watch you as you dream,
And morning holds the promise of another day's first gleam.
I am here,
And I am there,
And I am who I am.

His Faithfulness
Night Lights

"He stretches out the heavens like a canopy;
and spreads them out like a tent to live in...
Lift your eyes and look to the heavens:
Who created all these?
He who brings out the starry hosts one by one,
and calls them each by name.
Because of His great power and mighty strength
not one of them is missing."
~ Isaiah 40:22-26

There is no comparison to a star-filled night at the beach.
The city glow is left far behind, and the brilliance of the moon
spotlights the coast. There is a stillness that sets in as the sun
goes down. Tiny specks of light flicker through the dark sky.
The black night suddenly comes alive with radiant constellations.

The stars pour forth speech. The Lord calls each of them by
name. Because of His great power and mighty strength, not
one of them is missing. Not one is forgotten.

In our lives, there are times of confusion and darkness.
We cannot see what lies ahead or even the path of our feet.
However, it is during these times that the Lord provides
guidance. Perhaps it is in the words of a friend, the
encouragement of Scripture, or the twinkle of a star. The
Father provides a light. So do not lose your confidence.
Look for the small specks of guidance.

Around me falls the nighttime, and I barely see the shore.
I pause my heart, reflecting, sensing desperate need for more.
The darkening eve holds mysteries that I can't understand:
I see just where I am; and all I know, this patch of sand.
Life is often filled with times that make no sense to me…
As night surrounds, it swallows daylight's bright reality.
From where I stand, Lord, I can't trace the lines of sovereign hands,
And questioning soon takes the place of resting in your plans.
I try to walk…I cannot see…I search for guiding light.
And what You make so clear by day, I quickly doubt by night.

But in a moment all can change; I miss how You invade,
But in a moment all can change, and I can be remade.

I take my eyes off footsteps, breathe in deep, and tilt my head.
Heaven's splendor speaks elaborate love—the kind I've only read.
I stand in sudden wonder as Your beauty fills the sky
With light and color I have missed with head down walking by.
The Creator's glory shines in every little twinkling star;
The moon becomes a spotlight beaconing radiance from afar.
I hold my breath, eyes dance with awe, I bow my head in prayer.
"My God, this gift is undeserved—forever you will share?"

When walking with my head cast down, consumed by selfish ways,
I lift my eyes…and hear…and drink in all You have to say.
You, oh Lord, are faithful, bringing stars out one by one,
By name You call them forth, Your power complete in all You've done.
In the day Your warming light illumines every turn,
And in the night Your eloquence delights our hearts that burn.
By Your great strength the stars You made You hold there in their place.
I trust the same for me, for I've been showered with sheer grace.

His Family

A Family Tradition

"A new command I give you:
Love one another. As I have loved you,
so you must love one another.
By this all men will know that you are My disciples,
if you love one another."
~ *John 13:34-35*

We can tell a lot about people by looking at those they surround themselves with. Relationships point to people's character and give insight into their idea of faithfulness, commitment, and unconditional love. An observer of my life could learn the most about me by looking at those that constantly surround me—my family. It is nearly impossible for me to separate family time from the beach. For as long as I can remember, the two have always been a package deal. Walking down the beach the other day, I became acutely aware that many share the seashore as a common place to celebrate the blessings of family. I see groups uniformed in matching bathing suits. I see groups building sandcastles, laughing and enjoying each other's company. Others are chasing little ones dolled up in floppy hats.

Families stake out their territory up and down the beach. A dozen colorful chairs are set up each and every day, and each summer they are filled with families. Every summer, people gather on this tiny island and celebrate the blessing of simply being together. The beach invites us to practice a deeply cherished value…family.

Family members know everything about us, yet for some reason, they love us despite it all. They teach us that life is best lived with the music of laughter to accompany it. In a large family, cousins are more than just distant relatives—they are brothers and sisters. Families share a unique bond. Often, they have shared a common love for this place by the sea. Family teaches us not to take life so seriously, but to laugh and find joy in the small things. Family prepares us for the life that lies ahead and teaches us how to love unconditionally.

Sitting here in the sun, I realize that my family taught me how to love the beach. Most importantly, they taught me how to fall in love with my faith and adore the Creator of the ocean deep, every grain of sand, and my heart. This summer, I have learned a new definition of family. When the going gets rough, family reminds us that there is great beauty, even in rocky places. With them, I have learned that life is fragile and is to be held endearingly with two open hands. I have learned that the Lord did not make us for this world, and thus we will never find true satisfaction in it. My family has cultivated my heart and taught me to embrace life. They have stood on the sidelines so my faith alone would be my center, but they have also stood close enough to encourage my daily walk. The beach holds precious memories for my family and me.

My family gathers at the beach. We have met here for many years. Here we help each other to grow, here we learn to love, and here we embrace the blessings we have been given as a family. Looking down the beach, we see the same blessing unfolding for others again and again. Even the sandpipers celebrate being together as a family. The beach celebrates a bond that defines who we innately are. The beach celebrates family.

His Giving
With Love, from God

*"Every good and perfect gift is from above,
coming down from the Father of heavenly lights..."*
~ James 1:17

I have this fear of one day waking up as if it were just another day. I woke up this morning for sunrise and rolled out of bed well before the sun even hit the horizon. Noticing a line of clouds parading across the ocean, I determined that it probably would not be a sunrise worth the painful cost of a 6:15 rising. That is my fear: complacency. Waking up to another day. Waking up thinking that this day will be exactly like yesterday and no different from tomorrow.

Laziness tugs me back towards the dark room at the back of the house. I convince myself that the day can arrive without my assistance. The beginning does not rely on me, thank goodness.

Praise the Lord that He works even amidst our selfish desires. Something greater than my need for sleep kept me up this morning. Sitting in silence, with the stillness of the morning all around me, I waited for the first glimpse of another day. And that's when it happened. Coming from behind the clouds, the bright morning light shed golden rays on the tip of the formation, creating a golden crown on the horizon. With each passing moment, streaks of color burst from the crown, exploding in the sky and sending praise back to its source— the morning sun.

After more than twenty summers on this tiny island, it has become a great part of me. Naturally, I have grown to fear my complacency. But this morning I found myself taking countless pictures of the sunrise. With every degree of change, I snapped as though this was my first time to see such wonder—almost like it was my first day to be alive.

The extravagance of this morning awakened my heart to a voice I know in such a rare form of intimacy. *"My child,"* He *whispered, "today is a day unlike any other. It will not hold a candle to yesterday, nor will it rival tomorrow. It is a gift to be embraced this very moment, for soon time will pass and the gift will be gone. Today I will show you things you have never seen before. Today I will open your heart and stretch it in ways you never imagined. I need you to trust Me to do this according to My plan. For beloved, I promise to never lead My faithful servant astray. Every good and perfect gift flows directly from Me. Today is a gift and an opportunity to live in the present. Today is a day to live as if you never have before."*

My fear is that I will oversleep. My fear is that I'll roll over, see the clouds, and write this day off as just another. My fear is that I'll stop being a tourist. I'll awake someday to watch "yet another sunrise." Complacency is a great evil to be battled each and every day. But this morning, I made a promise I intend to forever keep. I will fight the urge of sleep when my heart calls me awake. I will greet the morning as if it were my first. I will allow my heart to be captivated by His grace, and I will pursue this day as if it were a gift. I will greet it as the first day of the rest of my life.

His Guidance

Burdens and Footprints

"Come to Me,
all you who are weary and burdened,
and I will give you rest.
Take My yoke upon you and learn from Me,
for I am gentle and humble in heart,
and you will find rest for your souls.
For My yoke is easy and My burden is light."
~ Matthew 11:28-30

I stand with my toes tucked in the sand. For the moment, the world has seemingly stopped around me. I am the only one who exists, and I am in the middle of a masterpiece created with me in mind. I have reached the end of the island, much like I have reached the end of my rope.

There is more beach ahead of me, but I have finally surrendered to the aching of my feet and the exhaustion of my body. I am tempted to continue on—pride tells me I can make it a bit further—but my heart calls me to sit and to be still. Gratefully, I claim a seat among shells, far enough from the surf's lingering line but close enough to catch its mist. Before me lies an old friend I have known for ages, a friend who shares my childhood and cherished memories. The Atlantic is calm today. Waves come in as steady swells, rising to their peak before racing onto the sand. Sea foam marks the surf and leaves the memory of a wave, but only for a moment. I stop here. I have nothing more to give to the journey ahead. I desperately try to take it all in, but somehow, that is impossible. I try to understand where I'm headed and how to get there, but that too seems impossible.

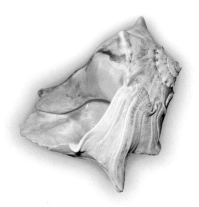

I notice the sandpipers running along the shoreline. They live day to day with unwavering faith. They trust their Creator to provide. Somehow, their faith is simple. I notice the consistency of the waves. They embody the consistency of their Master's grace. It does not matter what I do, or if I am not paying attention—I know they will keep rolling. I know they do not rely on me. I am captivated by the overwhelming beauty of the skies above the island. They exemplify their Maker's love. When I consider the work of His hand…the sun, stars, moon, and clouds that He has put into place…who am I that He is mindful of me?

I lose hope. My faith fails. I get caught in my own world of mundane clutter, yet the sunshine continues to warm me, and the stars continue to amaze me. I lose myself in the horizon. I struggle to see where it is leading and where the future may take me. I can never seem to grasp where it ends. No matter how hard I stare, and no matter how close I try to get, the line moves ahead, just far enough out of my reach. I lose perspective. I get frustrated thinking I have to know all the answers. I am tempted to see what the next step is. But I cannot know. All I know is that tomorrow morning the sun will peek over that line, my path will be lit, and my spirit will be renewed. I will be given just enough light for that day. Just when I think I will be given a preview of tomorrow, the sun will set, and I will be left with nothing but faith that it will rise again in the morning.

While planning ahead is important, each day demands my full attention. I do not want to miss what it holds or what Someone is anxious to show me. So I will be content in knowing that when night falls and I can no longer see the line ahead of me, I do not walk alone. I am given nightlights—brilliant stars to guide me through the dark until the morning leads me on. I do not know what the day will bring, but I do know Who created it. Somehow, that is enough. I may not understand why I need to travel this particular road. However, I realize that humility means sometimes not knowing, and that brings me back to this place in the sand.

I breathe in the salty air. I am exhausted from my journey but renewed from my stop. My heart stirs, and I regain perspective. The shore faithfully continues on, and I find the strength to follow its lead. I stand to collect my thoughts and feel the gentle kiss of the summer. I cling to the promise that His plan is great, and I walk on. With the wind at my back and sun on my face, I realize that this beach is my life, and I stand on nothing but its Maker's grace. He leads me beside quiet waters…He restores my soul…and I walk on…leaving nothing but burdens and footprints behind.

His Joy

Joyful Tidings

"Shout for joy to the Lord,
all the earth, worship the Lord with gladness;
come before Him with joyful songs.
Know that the Lord is God. It is He who made us,
and we are His; we are His people,
the sheep of His pasture.
Enter His gates with thanksgiving and
His courts with praise;
give thanks to Him and praise His name.
For the Lord is good and His love endures forever;
His faithfulness continues through all generations."

~ Psalm 100

I watched in fascination this morning as they made their way down the coastline. Though normally further out, this particular morning they followed the shore. Their friendly bob in and out of the water is always a sight to be seen. But this morning they not only requested our attention, they demanded it. Diving in and above the water, they proclaimed a greater joy than I have ever seen. With each leap and with every splash, they exclaimed the radiance of the morning light—proudly welcoming another day. Their parade of praise captivated an audience, eager to acclaim them for such splendor. Without hesitation, the dolphin's unspeakable, relentless joy shouted praise to a God who delights in such admiration.

To know joy temporarily is one thing, but to live a life defined by joy is quite another. We tend to know joy as an emotion—something that is dependent on the moment and affected by time and circumstance. We could learn a thing or two from dolphins of the great deep. For to them, joy is not a feeling; it is a lifestyle.

When "the joy of the Lord is your strength" (Nehemiah 8:10), it is evident in the way you live your life. And nothing honors the Father more than a life that holds His ministry as its purpose.

To have joy is to allow the spilling of our hearts to run over into the footprints of our lives. I have found that often the most inexpressible feeling is that of joy. What a wonderful predicament—not to know how to express the joyous swellings of the heart.

As believers, we are called to "be joyful always" (1 Thessalonians 5:16). While life is prone to lead us through valleys, we struggle for happiness and a skip in our step. But unlike the momentary satisfaction of happiness, joy does not change with circumstance. Rather, it reveals our very core and points to our true confidence.

When our cup overflows with the joy of the Lord, our lives cannot help but reflect it day after day. Watching the dolphins this morning, I did not question the God they serve. The joy in their leap revealed Him clearly. May we strive for a similar life—a life that exudes praise back to the Author and Perfector of our faith. May people look into our lives, notice the joy within us, and see a reflection of the Lord who moves our feet to dance and our hearts to praise.

His Legacy

Legendary: Following Footprints

"Gray hair is a crown of splendor;
it is attained by a righteous life."
~ Proverbs 16:31

The Lord is exemplified through the lives of His servants. We learn from the wisdom of those who set examples in our lives. My grandfather was the perfect example of a life lived for the glory of God. Papaw, as we called him, was larger than life. He loved us fully and completely. We spent every summer at the beach with Papaw. He taught us all to love the coastline and the golf course. He was the very essence of fatherly love as divinely designed.

Many people will come in and out of our lives. Some of them will breeze right by. But others will leave footprints for us to follow and learn from. These footprints can connect our thoughts and often answer our questions. The Lord's ministry is lived out through men and women who choose to lead lives of righteousness. Papaw lived that life. A life well lived leaves a legacy for generations to come. This poem was written in honor of the man who left footprints for my path.

This shoreline is covered with footprints,
Many that are bigger than my own.
I stroll their path as though following a map
And notice the distance they have traveled.
Each step is filled with history and wisdom from years gone by,
And they march forward with graceful assurance.

Your legacy, remembered here, has been our faithful guide;
Your life, a testament of love, in which we can confide.
Your footprints lead through times of joy and carry me through fear.
Your memory keeps me walking; in this place, I feel you near.
Your life has left a legacy.

These prints stretch into the distance
And soon fall out of sight.
I count the days till we meet again
But for now, I know my call…
To live a life that exudes His praise
And to leave a legacy for one to follow,
As I have followed yours.

Your legacy, remembered here, has been our faithful guide;
Your life, a testament of love, in which we can confide.
Your footprints lead through times of joy and carry me through fear.
Your memory keeps me walking; in this place, I feel you near.
Your life has left a legacy.

With each step I see your life and notice
That it points to Someone of greater fame.
Your path is marked with honor,
And it flows directly to a Heavenly call.
Your prints point to Him and bring Him praise...
It is my prayer that I may do the same.
A life of legacy is exactly what you accomplished—
And for that I will daily strive.

Your legacy, remembered here, has been our faithful guide;
Your life, a testament of love, in which we can confide.
Your footprints lead through times of joy and carry me through fear.
Your memory keeps me walking; in this place, I feel you near.
Your life has left a legacy.

I step in each print, though it is considerably bigger than mine.
And with each stride, I try to live as you did.
I strive to point to Him as I often saw you do…
With life, laughter, and unending love.
You lived as a servant to your family and your God.
His legacy is left behind in the lives of those faithfully called…
So when we walk, we should notice the prints we step in.

Your legacy, remembered here, has been our faithful guide;
Your life, a testament of love, in which we can confide.
Your footprints lead through times of joy and carry me through fear.
Using you, He's kept me walking; in this place, He's drawn us near.
Your life still speaks though you are gone, and we still celebrate.
Your legacy will be our lives until we're face to face.

His Love
Everlasting Love Story

"I have loved you with an everlasting love."
~ Jeremiah 31:3

I love to walk. I always have. I love taking off down the shoreline. North or south, it does not matter. With someone or by myself, it makes no difference. Just as long as I am barefoot, in the water…and walking. Low tide is an ideal time, for the beach is wide, and more shell pockets are exposed. The far south end of the island is renowned for beautiful sand dollars, though they are few and far between. It is a special occasion to find one in perfect condition. But I am convinced that the shells we find are the ones meant especially for us.

God is a true romantic. He knows precisely what captivates our hearts, for He fashioned them Himself. And He delights in stealing our breath away, in leaving us speechless, and in moving us to praise-filled tears. He displays His romantic character and His everlasting love as anyone would—He shows us and showers us with gifts. These gifts, however, do not come in the form of chocolates and flowers (though fields of wildflowers beg to differ). They come in sunsets, in star-filled skies, in animals, and in the simple radiance of shells.

His romancing, however, is immensely personal, designed to fit our hearts perfectly. The beauty of His creation is a daily reminder that He fashioned it and set it apart for His glory, and when He opens our eyes, we see His creation beckoning us also to be set apart for the One who has loved us. His is an intentional pursuit and a relentless chase with a passionate goal: capturing our hearts in a divine moment in time with His everlasting love.

For some of us, the mountains stir our hearts. The extravagance of mountainous creation draws out our deepest longings. And for some of us, the gentle serenity of the beach and of intricate shells awakens the very heartbeat of our souls. The Lord is an extravagant, intimate Lover who knows what makes us sing. Find what you deeply love…and then watch for God to move your heart in unpredictable ways.

During my last visit to this beach, I took a walk to the south end. Still in the early part of summer, the water was chilled. However, it was the perfect temperature to cool my feet. Lost somewhere in thought, I walked with my head down, watching each wave brush across my ankles and then retreat back to sea. Tiny sandpipers scurried ahead of me. O Lord, what joy is found in watching such frenzy! As I neared the Point—the place where the island ends—the beach seemed deserted, and the laughter of families was soon far behind me. Still, the water continued to glisten, the radiance of the sun continued to shine, and the soft sand continued to squish between my toes.

I was walking in a love story, and of all people, the main Character was pursuing me. Lavished with gifts from my Pursuer, I walked on feeling embraced by the Creator.

He had given me another day to walk with Him. He had sustained His loving handiwork for my joy and the praise of His glory. He is Someone who knows what I love and shows me in extravagance. At the climax of my heart's joyful song, I looked down to see a shape of familiarity and perfection. A sand dollar—tucked ever so slightly in the sand—grabbed my attention and shouted my name. There was no one else around. This shell was meant just for me.

The perfection of the Lord's timing is often hard to comprehend. He knew the precise day I would walk this beach and, since the beginning of time, He planned the exact moment when my feet would match the timing of the mighty ocean, and I would come in contact with such a magnificent creation. That sand dollar reminds me that our Lover is personal. He knows what we adore and loves us through those things. He ordains every moment to reflect His perfection. It was not a coincidence that I found a sand dollar that day. It was simply another example of a deeply committed God and an everlasting love story.

His Majesty

Remain Amazed

"*Look at the nations and watch—and be utterly amazed.
For I am going to do something in your days
that you would not believe, even if you were told.*"

~ Habakkuk 1:5

Early in the summer, when beachgoers are few and far between, I took a walk towards the north end of the island. Schools had not yet finished for the year, so the island seemed very much my own once more. Occasionally during my walk I would pass a fellow walker, exchange polite greetings, and then continue on. I was particularly taken with one woman I passed that day.

Standing knee high in the water, she must have been in her late seventies. Obviously a beach regular for years, she was gently weathered by time. She did not even notice my passing as she gazed into the water and over the horizon. Her focus fascinated me, though I thought nothing more of it...until I passed by an hour later on my return. Her stance, the same as when I had seen her before, now made perfect sense. It seems that she and I know the same secret about this tiny island. And such secrets captivate our attention and our very being. Such secrets leave us utterly amazed.

The most intimate form of worship, of course, varies from person to person. However, I am convinced that nothing exudes heartfelt praise like amazement. We worship the Lord with our amazement when our words fail. From the majesty of the mountains to the serenity of the sea, creation bellows for acclamation. But beyond words, beyond eloquent poetry and beautiful music, silent amazement speaks our deeply felt meditations.

Amazement is watching a sunrise and not being able to conjure up fitting words to describe the beauty we behold in the sky. Amazement is allowing the tranquility of a deserted beach to steal our breath away. We stand in silence as the surf tickles our toes. Amazement speaks right to the heart of our masterful Creator. He longs to hear our hearts echo, "Father, Your beauty leaves me speechless. Be magnified in my silence."

When we give a gift, we want the gift to take that special person's breath away. We want them to be amazed at our thoughtfulness. When they pause in silent amazement, when our hearts delight to see their response, this moment becomes a beautiful reminder that we are created in the very image of God. The Lord delights to give us staggering gifts that stop us in our tracks...amazed.

I am often without words when it comes to the beach, for it seems impossible to capture such beauty. So I must let amazement take over when my words fall short. No one understands our grateful hearts more than the One who fashioned them. Stand in awe and allow your heart to exclaim. Silence speaks beyond what words can communicate.

Though I never spoke to the woman that day, I knew we shared a kindred spirit. When creation celebrates, as it often does at the seashore, words are inadequate. But the Lord loves it when we are speechless, when all we can do is remain amazed.

His Peace

Pavilion of Peace

*"You will keep in perfect peace him whose mind
is steadfast, because he trusts in You."*
~ Isaiah 26:3

The peace of the Lord is a remarkable experience. Life is
turbulent. There are moments of confusion and unsteadiness.
But in the midst of such disconnects, the peace of the Lord
stands strong. I have walked through times when my faith was
the only thing that made sense to me. My world seemed
dim and full of snares. It was during those times that I truly
understood the sweetness of heavenly peace. The Lord's
faithfulness is steadfast. His peace rains down when the storms
of life are marked with intensity.

As I walk the shore, I notice beach pavilions along the way.
Families set up tents to shade them from the sun and mark
their spot. Pavilions provide protection from harmful rays.
Similarly, God provides a pavilion of peace to guard us against
life's most blistering spots. We are shaded from harm
and comforted in our deepest needs. The peace of the Lord
continues to transcend my every understanding.

do not know the road ahead,
And today's path I can barely see.
The life ahead is a mystery beyond my understanding,
And I don't know the plans You have laid
But deep within this wandering heart,
There is a calmness that excites my innermost thoughts.
You pavilion my soul with peace.

I do not understand Your ways
Or why You work the way You do.
From my point of view, these trials do not make sense,
For they often hurt and cause my heart to ache.
But I know Your thoughts are higher than mine.
You pavilion my soul with peace.

I live in this world that is so far from You,
And it seems so separated from Your touch.
Day by day You renew my spirit
And lift my sights on high.
I trust in Your providence and a greater purpose.
You pavilion my soul with peace.

I sit on this beach with the weight of the world on my mind.
Before me the ocean sings, and it calls to me something deep.
I take note of each wave's assurance and its steady roll.
The simplicity of the tide challenges the complexity of my mind,
And I know Your ways are greater than mine.
You pavilion my soul with peace.

I celebrate my life thus far,
Reflecting on each memory past.
I miss those that have gone before and struggle to set my sights on high.
Though my heart knows the truth,
My head searches for answers that are not mine to know.
But You have spoken truth to my longing heart
And promised a reunion that will be grand.
You pavilion my soul with peace.

You are the Author and Revealer of mystery,
So today's mysteries I'd rather leave to You.
They keep me wandering back to my Peace.
You often call me again to this beach,
And I have no idea what to expect from this day,
But I will fully trust in Your provision.
The songs of Your creation echo truth,
And the steps of my life reflect Your plan of perfection.
You pavilion my soul with peace.

His Perfect Timing

Perfect Timing

*"O Lord, You are my God; I will exalt You and praise
Your name, for in perfect faithfulness You have done
marvelous things, things planned long ago."*
~ Isaiah 25:1

How does the pelican know the precise moment a wave will
curl? How does the bird glide inches above the wave's
ever changing shape? With an unexplainable grace, the pelican
moves above the water and along the waves with confidence.
His timing is perfect.

How does the sandpiper scurry along the shore, perfectly
outlining the wave's wandering line? He comes within
centimeters of being swept away by the water's ebb and flow,
and yet his timing, as well, is seemingly perfect.

How does the sea turtle know to come ashore and bury her
eggs? Why, weeks later, in a single moment, does each and
every egg swell with life just before hundreds of hatchlings
race for the sea? How do they know to go all at once? How is
their timing altogether perfect?

The timing of creation is a reflection of the timing of its
Creator. In perfect faithfulness, He succeeds in marvelous
things. And those things know perfection in timing, for they
were planned long ago.

We are quick to take matters into our own hands. We convince ourselves that, unless we take initiative, things will not work out; and certainly our timing will be far from perfect.

Somehow this world has led us to believe that planning ahead is everything, as if an organized lifestyle and an ambitious plan are what we need to ensure success on the road ahead. In the midst of the world's pressures to achieve, we can rest in the Lord's perfect timing. We remember that we can be successful in the world's eyes and unfaithful to the Lord. We can watch all our plans fail in the world and still rest in His perfect timing.

I have known a valley. I have known what it feels like to be lost in myself and unable to see the road ahead of me. Perhaps thoughts of utter helplessness and frustrating confusion have held us all captive. Striving to move forward, it is easy to be slowed down with a lack of self-confidence. However, though pressed on every side, we are never crushed. The Lord's timing sings of perfection. "He set my feet on a rock and gave me a firm place to stand. He put a new song in my mouth, a hymn of praise to our God" (Psalm 40:2-3).

Timing, we are told, is everything. But not our own timing. Our Father knows when to clear the clouds and shower us with sunshine. He knows what we need and the precise moment we need it. What is more, He knows the meditations of our hearts and instills desires with great purpose.

Rest in the callings of your heart. Do not ignore them—consult them carefully—and trust in a timing that has been planned specifically with you in mind. "Many, O Lord my God, are the wonders You have done. The things You planned for us no one can recount to You; were I to speak and tell of them, they would be too many to declare" (Psalm 40:5).

When you question the timing of the Creator, look at His creation. The pelican knows the precise timing of the curl. The sandpiper understands the pattern of the shoreline. And collectively, hundreds of sea turtles know the month, week, day, hour, and exact moment to crawl from their nest. They faithfully follow the moon and scramble towards the sea. "Are you not much more valuable than they?" (Matthew 6:26). Your heavenly Father knows what you need, and what is more, He knows when you need it. We serve an unfathomable God who, in perfect faithfulness, shows us His perfect timing.

His Preparation
Summer's End

"There is a time for everything and a
season for every activity under heaven:
a time to be born and a time to die,
a time to plant and a time to uproot,
a time to tear down and a time to build,
a time to weep and a time to laugh,
a time to mourn and a time to dance,
a time to embrace and a time to refrain…"
~ Ecclesiastes 3:1-5

The end of summer comes like an afternoon thunderstorm on the beach. It is never planned, always unexpected, always pulling me off the beach and sending me home. I was on the southernmost tip of the island when it hit yesterday. Naturally, I was unprepared. Clouds had been gathering throughout the morning, so I knew the inevitable. But I walked on, hoping that the storm would never come. At the very least, I could ignore it for a while and stay on the beach. I never know when it is going to hit…and it never comes when I'm ready. The dark clouds tumble over the blue sky. I do my best to walk forward, pretending it is not looming over my head. In the distance, thunder rumbles, and occasionally lightning illuminates the horizon. And then, as though having my permission, the storm invades my paradise and sends me back home.

I've learned that coastal storms are very similar to the end of summer. For nine months, I wait in anxious anticipation for those three precious months to arrive. Finally, school is done, the air is a little lighter, and the blessed months of wonderful summer are upon us. Summer is a time of immense growth and powerful restoration. I bask in the sun, trying desperately to make it last. My days are filled with family chaos, sunbathing, and unending sunshine. I grow so accustomed to being here at the beach that returning home is a foreign thought. This island has the ability to allure my heart, and

through my time here, the Lord captivates my soul. This summer, I have been taught the blessing of the Lord's restoration. His quiet waters have cleansed my soul, and the hunger I felt all year is satisfied. As well as I know this place, it is still a mystery to me. I can never fully grasp it. The beauty I see and the emotions that tug at my heart can never be contained. When I go home, the mystery remains. More thoughts, more growth for another time.

Before I know it, the dark clouds begin to form, a storm rolls in, and summer comes to a close. I wait it out as long as possible. Not wanting to give up the sun, I dread the thought of bidding farewell to my beloved beach. But summer is coming to a close, the rain gently begins to fall, and home calls me back. The thoughts of responsibility, commitment, and a schedule are overwhelming, and I fight the urge to ignore it all. Surely the Lord can run His world without my help.

But who am I to hide this restored heart and not show it to a lost world? My time here has been a time of extreme rejuvenation and sweet silence. I have come to know my Creator and His majesty on an unprecedented level. And as a believer, I am called to "go"—to share such joy with the nations.

My time at the end of the island was the sweetest time I have ever known. Through tears of joy and bittersweet sadness, I watched the ocean roll and felt the gentle brush of the wind's touch on my face. In a moment of sudden conviction, I realized that this big blue expanse does not rely on me. In a day I will not be here, and I know that the waves will crash and the shells will scatter. I also realized that the kingdom's advance does not depend on me, but the King has graciously chosen me to be His ambassador. He desires to shine His Son's light through me to a world otherwise living in darkness. And what good does a hidden candle do? The Lord has lit my flame, and His plan does not call me to stay on an island. It calls me to the mainland.

O Lord, help me to make sense of this time of leaving. I long to stay in the beauty of this place. But You have restored me, so I will go. You have abundantly provided so that my cup will overflow and Your world will see a light. And so I will go. I will listen to the voice that calls me home, and I will tell of the great God that You are—Maker of the sea, Creator of its inhabitants. And the waves will roll, the sun will shine, and I will be back when the sweet scent of another summer is in the air. Prepare me as I go forth. Spill out of me as I leave, and reach a world through the restoration You have done in my heart.

I look behind me, and the storm is rolling in. Another day has ended, and another summer is coming to a close. It is time to head home, for the rain has started to fall. But I take comfort in knowing that there is a time for everything, a season for every activity under heaven. And it is time to go in. Summer is drawing to a close. The rain pushes me out of my place of complete contentment into a world that is desperate to know what I have been privileged enough to learn. Walking back down the beach, I leave tears and footprints behind and carry precious shelled memories in my hand. And the rain begins to fall—it is time to go home.

His Serenity

Seashore Serenity

"He leads me
beside quiet waters,
He restores my soul."
~ Psalm 23:2

The world that we live in is in a
constant state of panic.
Schedules dominate daily lives,
and checking off to-do lists
brings a sense of ultimate
satisfaction. Life is rush hour—
cars in traffic, horns and sirens
breaking any glimmer of silence,
and the tyranny of the urgent
causing our blood pressure to
rise. With life moving so fast, we
are constantly in danger of
missing something grand when
we don't stop to take it in. I have
learned that the greatest things
happen off the coast of
somewhere beautiful.

There is unparalleled tranquility
by the seashore. During the year,
it seems like only a fabrication
of our imagination. However, the
sweetness of summertime brings
most things into glorious reality.

Here, the world seems to slow its pace. We leave the stresses of everyday life on the mainland, and we taste true serenity with our toes in the sand and shells in hand. Here, the air is a bit lighter, and life's pathway is just a little bit brighter.

There are times in our lives when the clouds are too heavy to see through. We feel like, in every area of our lives, we are falling short. Tired of settling for complacency in the fast lane, our hearts beg to be restored to the place of absolute peace. I have known such a time. It was a time of dryness and confusion, and I certainly could not trace the meaning in what the Lord was doing. It was a time of sculpting and shaping. I just held on, trusting His hand to be the Potter's. And in the midst of such confusion came the beach—where quiet waters and restoration are unfathomable. Quiet waters…exactly what I needed to see. Restoration…exactly what my soul longed for.

Here on the beach, things come into perspective. I become much more aware that I must listen to and trust the callings of my heart. The Lord gives me time to think and fresh air to breathe.

Walks on the beach bring this kind of new perspective. I walk for hours on end, yet I never tire, and my soul never feels so alive. The scattering of each wave, the comforting warmth of each ray—my heart takes flight, and things fall into place. I watch my footprints in the sand, and while I see only one set, I know I am being carried.

Day after day, restoration comes, and my heart learns again how to see with perspective and trust with unwavering faith. The quiet waters minister to the calamity within me.

There is a great serenity on the shore, an unmatched sensation that reaches our hearts. Here His path is straight, and our vision is clear. And step by step, the footprints stretch into the horizon, and our souls can know true restoration.

His Splendor

An Artist's Splendor

"The heavens declare the glory of God;
the skies proclaim the work of His hands. Day after day they
pour forth speech; night after night they display knowledge.
There is no speech or language where their voice
is not heard. Their voice goes out into all the earth,
their words to the ends of the world."

~Psalm 19:1-4

His palate is filled with the perfect combination of vibrant colors—red, orange, pink, yellow, and a hint of purple. His selection of brushes varies in size, shape, and texture, but it is obvious they each have their specific purpose. The canvas in front of Him is blank, void of color and life, but He has a twinkle in His eye that fills me with wonder. He has the perfect picture in mind.

His hands are worn with age and time—each wrinkle a sign of wisdom. They exude a sense of confidence and stability. It is clear He has experience. This masterpiece is not His first. He quickly goes to work. First, selecting a thin, light brush, He streaks the blank canvas with gentle hues of pink and soft oranges. Continuing with this brush, He gradually adds more color, and the shades begin to intensify.

As He changes His brush, He moves at a hurried pace, but with a sense of grace that is strangely melodic. Reaching for the thickest brush, He begins to blend the paint to create a color that fills me with memories of a place I have known since childhood. He selects the boldest colors of radiant red and brilliant yellow. Now moving in a frenzy, colors begin to splash, and I lose track of His pattern. His pace is frantic; His expression peaceful. He smiles, and His eyes gleam with excitement and assurance. I can tell He has done this before, but that this particular creation is a new pattern.

Colors fly and I am quickly blinded by the brightness of the canvas. I stand in amazement as He caresses the masterpiece before Him. There is a moment of inexplicable joy drawn from my heart as I watch Him pour color onto the scene that is now exploding with His passion.

Suddenly, He slows down and selects soft colors that soon blend into a mixture. The canvas begins to soften with shades of purple and blue. He is calm, yet still gleaming with excitement. His eyes speak of accomplishment. Turning around, He smiles as I have never seen before.

"Beloved, the heavens declare my glory; the skies proclaim the work of my hands. Day after day, night after night, they pour

forth speech. And all the world can see and hear it. Do you like it? I thought of you as I worked and knew that it would be the perfect expression of your heart and My love for you. I created this piece so that you would remember that I have something wonderful planned for you. When you look at this canvas, know that it declares the work of My hands and the glory of My kingdom. Night after night, I'll be here painting another reminder of My promise and filling you with knowledge of one of My true passions—you.

"I will be here every day, around the same time, creating something perhaps similar, but never the same. You are welcome to watch Me as I work, but you must strive to make time. This is an event I want to share with you because there is so much I want to show you. I have selected colors that represent so many things that are precious to you. And though the world may see it on display, this painting is uniquely personal to you. It is a representation of something that only you and I share.

"Take this canvas and hang it on the walls of your heart, for tomorrow's will not be the same. I have something incredible in mind for tomorrow, and I would love to share that with you. I'll see you then—you know where to find Me."

With that, He turned back around and began to clean up His area. Before I left, I noticed He had already put another blank canvas on the easel, perhaps for tomorrow. My heart still racing with excitement, I left His workshop. Looking down at the canvas in my hand, I laughed with anxious anticipation of meeting Him tomorrow evening. And so I strolled quietly down the beach, carrying a canvas sunset in my hands and watching the same scene splash across the sky.

His Stillness
Stillness

"Be still and know that I am God;
I will be exalted among the nations,
I will be exalted in the earth."
~ *Psalm 46:10*

Life seems so simple by the seashore.
Moments go by and it seems as though the
rest of the world has stopped, and all that
remains is a tiny island in the middle of a vast
expanse.

Life seems so chaotic back home. The
demands of another workday weigh us down,
and the rest of the world races by without
so much as a glimpse in our direction. It is
rush hour, we are late, and the to-do list runs
forever on.

I often find myself busy—but in all the wrong
areas. I am quick to volunteer and commit,
and I feel the pressure to achieve. Like
everyone else, I long for a free moment, time
to catch my breath. But the pressure to
maintain my pace makes me feel as though
fighting for stillness would be a waste of
energy. Stillness does not seem productive.

Life calls me to run, to be proactive, and to
stay busy. Life, I'm told, is a race, and only
the qualified and accomplished finish first.

Over time, I have come to realize that life is in fact a race. However, it is a race to chase after the glory of God. It is a race to reach eternity. But somewhere in between birth and eternity is this phenomenon called "life," and its goal is to discover how to run as efficiently as possible.

In this race called life, I keep my eyes focused on the goal and I notice my form. It is not a sprint…life is a marathon. In order to run well, we must plan on stopping for periodic maintenance.

True, at times we must push hard. As believers we are called to reach the nations with heavenly purpose. Reaching the four corners, however, requires a strength that does not come from activity. It is found in the stillness of His presence.

It is essential, then, that we rest and take time to let Him restore us. We need time to know the doctrine of our faith and to be in tune with the Lord. Nothing speaks to the stillness of the Lord like the serene ambiance of the shoreline. Creation stills, waves bring heaven-sent reassurance, and the soul is stimulated beyond earth's realms.

The beach is not just a vacation; it is an escape from the shouts of this world into the silent whispers of the Lord. Laden with burden and exhausted, I arrive at the island in broken pieces. Head spinning with demands and emotional baggage, the weight of life sinks me into the sand.

But oh the sweet stillness that sweeps in through an ocean breeze! There is something frightfully powerful in the call of the sea. The extravagance of the mighty waves and the simplicity of their gentle touch leave no room for the world's frantic thoughts. In a matter of moments, creation has swept over my soul. It beckons me to sit, to cry, to pray, to rejoice, and to drop my burdens one by one by one.

A brush with our Creator is an encounter unlike any other. He summons us to His creation and makes us lie down in green pastures. He asks us to stop, pull over, and be restored. He provides a place, a time, and a plan for our restoration. And best of all, as we learn to be still before Him, He graces us with a deeper awareness of His presence.

And in those moments, as I meet with Him, I am restored. I leave the seashore equipped to run for His glory. I turn and look behind me at the serenity that pours forth from every angle and exclaims, *"Be still, My beloved, and know that I alone am God."*

His Teaching
Sleepless Mornings

"He wakens me morning by morning,
wakens my ear to listen like one being taught."
~ *Isaiah 50:4*

There is something divine about mornings at the beach. They are quiet. They are mysterious. They are full of teachable moments. While you are at the beach, set your mind on waking up before anyone else. Sit in the stillness of the dawn and listen. The Lord teaches through His creation. And in the mornings there are few distractions. Your mind is clear, and the chaos of the approaching day has yet to arrive.

This particular morning, I awoke well before the sun. This poem was the song of my heart.

Lord, I cannot sleep this morning,
Though my body is worn from the day past.
My soul is wide awake with joy,
My heartbeat increasingly fast.
You awaken me morning by morning
And call me to quietly sit.
You awaken my heart to listen…
Showing me the plan You perfectly knit.
So here I am, Lord, quiet,
I'm awaiting what You'll say.
A lifted heart, a bended knee—
Father, speak to me today.

Have you ever considered that Jesus understands our daily battle to slow down, to fight the noise, to listen for the still small voice? Life was no less chaotic for Jesus during his years on earth. Imagine all the demands and expectations placed on one with power to work miracles and insight to teach with authority. We quickly think that if anyone could survive without a time alone with the Lord, Jesus could. He was fully man and fully God, and yet the gospels remind us: "Very early in the morning, while it was still dark, Jesus got up, left the house and went off to a solitary place, where He prayed" (Mark 1:35).

Where did He go? Perhaps to the shores of the Sea of Galilee. What did He pray? Perhaps that the Father would bring glory to His name through the Son and that the Son would have everything He needed to obey the Father. His Father wakened Him morning by morning, and He listened like one being taught. He is our hope and our guide, and in His time on earth and by His Spirit now, He leads us into the presence of the Father who teaches His children on sleepless mornings. Arise and go to your Father.

His Welcoming Heart

Welcome Home

"Let the name of the Lord be praised,
both now and forevermore.
From the rising of the sun, to the place where it sets,
the name of the Lord is to be praised."

~ Psalm 113:2-3

It is the feeling I get when I step off the plane, the beat of my heart as we drive down the highway and cross the bridge hitting the island. In less than a minute, the mainland is behind me and my tiny island is standing before me with its arms wide open. It is the rush of adrenaline when I hear the roar of the ocean. It is the peace I feel when I finally see it with my own eyes. It is letting my hair blow in the salty sea breeze and allowing it to carry every care in the world away from me. It is releasing my spirit, handing over my heart to this old familiar place. No, it is not just a vacation. It is certainly not just an island. This is home.

Leaving the beach at the end of summer has always been a struggle for me. But the more I think about it, the more I realize that such emotions are only natural when I am leaving so much of my heart behind. Returning to this place by the sea, my heart is returning home. For years, I have walked this shoreline, and through those years, I have learned life's greatest lessons. In a world of chaos, the beach is one of our Creator's ways of proclaiming faithfulness, simplicity, and a plan that far exceeds our expectations.

Suddenly, I am swept into a world that is beyond the one we live in. It is an escape from reality, a trip to the most treasured and hidden places of who we innately are. Life's lessons must be lived, not simply observed. And here, away from the clutter of our daily lives, is the perfect place to begin.

I close my eyes and breathe deeply the air I have so desperately needed. The palm trees whistle, and that old friend rolls on wave by wave by wave. This is where the sun will rise in the morning and where it will set in the evening—and my soul will proclaim the glory of the Lord. I open my eyes and celebrate that this is not just a dream. This is life. There is not a sound around me that could pull my attention away from my focus. The ocean roars, the wind sings, and all of creation whispers...

"Welcome Home."